SPACE
CLEARING

SPACE
CLEARING

harmonize your home for mind, body & soul

EMILY CLAYTON

THUNDER BAY
P·R·E·S·S

San Diego, California

Thunder Bay Press

An imprint of the Advantage Publishers Group
5880 Oberlin Drive, San Diego, CA 92121-4794
www.thunderbaybooks.com

All notations of errors or omissions should be addressed to
Thunder Bay Press, Editorial Department, at the above address. All other correspondence
(author inquiries, permissions) concerning the content of this book should be addressed to
Salamander Books Ltd, 8 Blenheim Court, Brewery Road, London, N7 9NY, U.K.

ISBN 1-57145-957-X
Library of Congress Cataloging-in-Publication Data available upon request.

Printed in China
1 2 3 4 5 07 06 05 04 03

Credits

EDITOR: Katherine Edelston
DESIGNER: Claire Graham
PRODUCTION: Don Campaniello
COLOR REPRODUCTION: Anorax
PRINTED AND BOUND IN CHINA

Contents

Introduction

Space is a very precious commodity and everyone, at some point in their lives, has decided that they need more of it. But, more often than not, the problem is not so much lack of space as that the available space is filled with clutter. This applies not only to the physical space around you, but also to your mental space. Clutter, in whatever form it takes, prevents you from moving forward. Clearing space raises the energy surrounding you, helping to change your life fundamentally and allowing you to experience a more positive, healthier, and happier lifestyle. It will help you harmonize yourself, your home, and your workplace to enhance love, increase prosperity, and boost health and vitality for all the occupants.

Contemporary life is very stressful and the home should be a sanctuary; somewhere you can relax, shrug off the tensions of the day just passed, and prepare for the day to come. But the home also has another essential function—it is a storage place for most of the necessary possessions of modern-day life. Centuries ago, a person could store all their worldly possessions in one box, but this is no longer possible for most of us, nor would we wish it to be. However, the sheer weight of "belongings" must not be allowed to overwhelm the space available for them. Using simple organization techniques and carrying out regular and ruthless pruning will keep things under control and create a home that will function as a support system, rather than requiring support itself.

When the energy within your home or workplace is out of sync, life can become disorganized on a great many levels, leaving you feeling drained, disenchanted, and ill. Developing a much better understanding of the energetic environments in which we all live and understanding how the subtle energies within our homes or working environments can affect our ability to function efficiently is one of the first steps to achieve lasting success. Using simple feng shui techniques will improve your environment, increase your prosperity, and enhance your personal relationships. Studying and rationalizing flow patterns will improve how the space is used, and carefully-placed wind chimes, mirrors, and crystals will divert negative energy away and enhance the positive influences. Even just adding different or more color can change the whole feeling and ambience of a room and the way you interact with it.

On a personal level, it is important to learn to recognize and tune into your aura, activate your chakra system, and sense the energy force all around you. Using crystals, smudge sticks, candles, salt, essential oils, and flower remedies, as well as various simple meditation

Clearing space raises the
energy around you,
helping to change your life
fundamentally.

"The *body* is the tree of enlightenment,
The *mind* is like a bright mirror-stand.

Wipe it clean over and over

and do not let the dust alight."

SHEN-HSUI

techniques, will clear space in your mind. This will enable you to develop your own mind power and start learning to use positive thinking, stress-busting techniques, and simple relaxation exercises that will help to improve your everyday performance.

Many people find that they seem to be unable to move forward in life, but do not really know why. Utilizing a few simple "life coach" techniques will help you identify the block, and suggest ways to move around it. It can also help you focus on what you really want in life and start moving you toward it in small and manageable steps.

We can't all be spiritual all the time—but making space in your life both physically and mentally will allow you to be yourself, and will open up wonderful new vistas for you to enjoy.

PART ONE

Cleansing the Environment

CHAPTER ONE

An Introduction to Space Clearing

No matter how careful we are, possessions accumulate. Perhaps the first impulse as we become overwhelmed is to find a bigger home, but a simpler and cheaper solution is to reorganize or clear away what we have. Many of us are no longer aware of exactly what we own—everyone has something tucked away in a dark corner or hidden at the back of the cupboard that they have totally forgotten about!

It is not necessary to be rigidly disciplined or fanatical about tidiness to have a well-organized home. Simply by following a practical and commonsense approach, and including adaptable systems that can cope with changing circumstances, you can live much more efficiently with the minimum of effort. The first step is to analyze your needs honestly, identifying what you use most often and what you really do not need at all.

Although at first changes may have to be fairly major to make a difference, after the first thrust just a small amount of regular maintenance will be sufficient to keep things on an even keel. When you recapture that lost feeling of spaciousness in your home you will begin to enjoy your surroundings far more—and you will almost certainly find that it will also improve your whole life.

The paperless office is a myth.

KEEPING things you
DO NOT WANT
is wasteful—they take up
VALUABLE SPACE.
If you really can't bear to
THROW THEM AWAY,
DONATE THEM
to a charity shop.

If you recycle things you no longer want
or need, they may find a new home
with someone else who needs them.

"our
dream
home is always
larger than
the one we
live in"

Good organization oils the wheels of domestic life and makes the most of available space.

Clinging to your

clutter means that

you are clinging

to your past.

Learn to let go, and
move into the future
with a new, light step.

Things that you no longer need
are occupying valuable space that
could be put to better use.

Keeping your home clean and clutter-free reduces the risk of negative energy collecting.

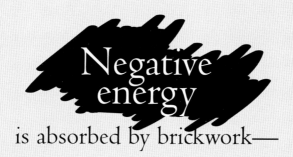

Negative energy is absorbed by brickwork— it clings to buildings and adversely affects all those inside.

Space clearing
and removing clutter
can be liberating.

Clinging onto
your past life can be
one of the signs
of depression.

Let go...

Most of us have

more space

than we think we do.

Space

clearing prepares

the building for

feng shui,

which works at

a deeper level.

CHAPTER TWO

Clearing Out & Creating Order

With the best will in the world, you are unlikely to clear our your entire home in a day. Just looking at the amount to be done over such a large area would probably daunt the most enthusiastic convert to decluttering. The key is to tackle things in manageable sections—large enough to make a difference, but small enough to be covered in one hit.

Pick a suitable time—ideally when you will be uninterrupted for long enough to do the job thoroughly. There are also certain times when a clear-out is easier—the beginning of winter is a better time to go through winter clothes than the end of the season, as you will not have worn them for some time and can be more objective. Times of general change are also ideal for a good throw-out—when you are about to move, redecorate, or just reorganize the rooms.

Too much clutter in your life not only fills it up, it can also waste your valuable time and increase your levels of frustration. It is much easier to find what you want among a few possessions in the right place, than by searching through a whole load of things that you have kept "just in case." However small the start, just get going, as the end result will benefit your entire life.

Get rid of anything that you have NOT WORN *for more than two seasons,* *or that is* UNCOMFORTABLE *or* *that does* NOT FIT.

If you buy something
new, *throw something*
old away as soon as
you get home.

If it has been broken for
more than 12 months, throw it away
—if you have managed without
it for that long,
you don't need it.

If you have duplicates
of anything, only keep
the newest or the one that
works the best.

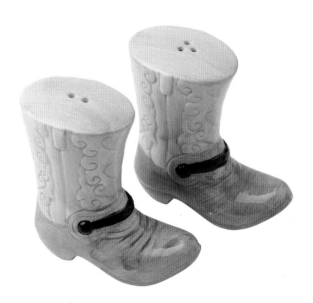

*Get rid of anything that you
have been given, but do not like.
You won't like it any better
in a few years.*

Collect all the equipment you need for a specific activity together. If you no longer do that activity, sell the items to someone who does.

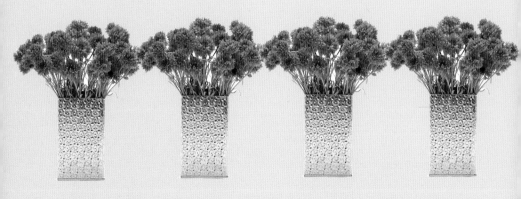

As you sort out your possessions,
reassess how you need them
and decide on the most efficient
place to store them.

Don't try to do
too much at once.
Start small and work
up to the bigger things.

Put anything you are not sure about into a box

at the back of a cupboard. If you haven't taken it out

of the box within six months,

you don't need it...

Dispose of the box without opening it.

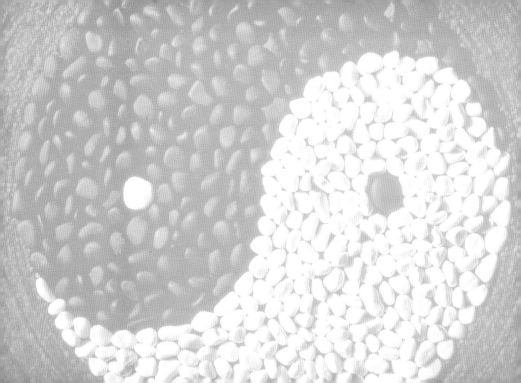

CHAPTER THREE

An Introduction to Feng Shui

The art of feng shui goes back over 3,500 years and has its roots in the Chinese way of looking at the world and categorizing everything into five elements: fire, metal, earth, wood, and water. In addition, everything has either yin or yang energy. The practice of feng shui consists of balancing the five elements and the yin and yang, and correcting disharmony in the home so that health, happiness, and good fortune come to everyone who lives there. A mystique sometimes surrounds feng shui, but it is not a religion and you do not have to believe in it for it to work. As long as your analysis of your home or workplace is firmly based on the theories that underpin the system, feng shui will work for you. Since it offers so much for so little effort, it is worth trying however you feel about it.

Feng shui does not have to be difficult to practice—many of its principles are common sense. It is almost impossible to have perfect feng shui—a key principle is to work with what you have. Good feng shui brings opportunities, enhances living conditions, and creates goodwill in relationships. Although it cannot create instant good fortune, it works steadily over time to increase the favorable energy around the home and protect it from bad influences.

Each compass point relates to one of
the five elements. Placing that element in the
corresponding sector of your home will
energize that sector.

	N	NE
NW METAL	**N** WATER	**NE** EARTH
W METAL	EARTH	**E** WOOD
SW EARTH	**S** FIRE	**SE** WOOD

THE FIRE ELEMENT

Fire is associated with the south. When the south
is energized it brings success and fame. Since fire itself
may be difficult to create in the right sector, it can be
symbolized by a bright light, burning candle, or the
color red. Wood is also good to energize the
south sector, as wood fuels fire.

THE WOOD ELEMENT

Wood is associated with the east and southeast. When the east is energized it brings good health, while energizing the southeast brings wealth. Use any kind of plant or flower, except dried ones, cactus, or stunted bonsai trees. Water is also good to energize the east and southeast sectors, as water fuels wood.

THE WATER ELEMENT

Water is associated with the north. When the north is energized it brings good luck in your career. A good way of introducing the water element is to install an aquarium. Water can also be symbolized by using blue or black colors in the decor.

THE METAL ELEMENT

Metal is associated with the west and northwest.
When energized in the west it brings good luck to the children
of the household and in the northwest it represents the
presence of mentors to help you on your way. A pot
of gold or a handful of coins are two of the best
representations of metal.

THE EARTH ELEMENT

Earth is associated with the southwest and northeast
and center sectors. When energized in the southwest it brings
love and marriage, and in the northeast it represents
education. Energizing the center of the home will
bring harmony and good fortune to the whole family.
Both ceramics and crystals can be used to
energize earth sectors.

Symbols of
good fortune
are an important part
of feng shui and they
should be displayed in the home
so that they blend in with
the decor and are not
too obvious.

Before placing them in your home,
the symbol should be washed clean of
negative energies, using salted water
or sea salt. The simplest way of
energizing the symbol is to
tie a length of red thread
or ribbon to it.

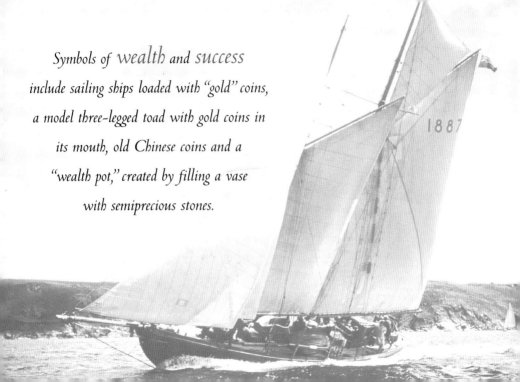

Symbols of wealth and success
include sailing ships loaded with "gold" coins,
a model three-legged toad with gold coins in
its mouth, old Chinese coins and a
"wealth pot," created by filling a vase
with semiprecious stones.

Symbols of longevity and
health include the crane, the pine tree,
bamboo, the peach, and Sau,
the god of longevity.

Symbols of LOVE and HAPPY marriage
include the peony, a pair of mandarin ducks, and
the Chinese sign for double happiness.

*Symbols of protection
include the tiger,
the eagle, the fan, and
the Fu dog.*

CHAPTER FOUR

Cleansing your Space

Sometimes our homes seem full of stale, negative energy and this will have a big impact on how we feel. If your house is quiet and empty during the day while you are out at work, it will have too much yin energy when you return, making the occupants feel lethargic and tired. When moving into a new home, you will have to contend with the "atmosphere" left by the previous occupant, whether this is good or bad. A death in the building can leave a massive build-up of negative energy that is difficult to deal with unless the space is properly cleansed afterward.

Feng shui offers several ways of identifying and dealing with such problems, with techniques that concentrate on either deflecting, dissolving, or balancing out the negative forces, and cleansing the space to allow positive energy to flourish. Even if you have been in the same home for many years, changes happen over time, so you may find that something that has worked well is now going wrong. This may be due to passing bad luck, to something that has been changed within the home, or to something different outside—a new building or element that has changed the flow of chi, or energy coming toward the house. If such changes can be identified and dealt with quickly, the negative energy will not have time to cause major problems.

If you have a run of bad luck,
or if members of your family continually
fall ill, one after another, then start
by cleansing your home of negative
chi before trying to activate
any of the sectors with
feng shui techniques.

Make sure you carry out the cleansing when you are feeling happy and positive, or you will risk adding further negative energy layers.

*When a room feels stale
and lifeless or has not been used
for some time, there is a
lack of fresh chi.*

Open both *window* and *door* in the room to be cleansed, to encourage a flow of *air* and allow fresh *chi* to enter.

Dark areas and corners are where negative chi tends to build up.

Clean the room thoroughly,
making sure to remove any
debris from corners and
behind furniture.

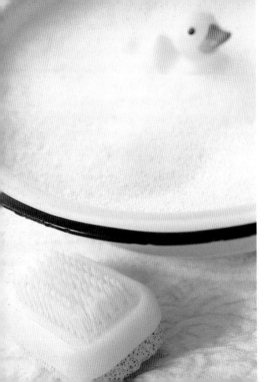

Rooms that have
an unhappy atmosphere
should be cleansed
before trying to
energize them.

Incense or scented candles should be used to dispel unhappy feelings. Lavender *and sage are particularly effective.*

Movement is very beneficial to increase yang energy and remove negative chi, either dancing or moving round rhythmically while singing or chanting.

Homes left empty
all day suffer from
excessive yin energy.

Silence will also cause excessive *yin* energy—which is fine in a bedroom but *enervating* in the living areas.

Use sound to energize the space—play classical music or clapping rhythms. Striking a tuned bell or a singing bowl is also effective. Homes full of the sound of children or animals are naturally energized.

Dark corners or
gloomy rooms are places
where negative energy
will collect.

Bright lights, candles, or lamps will dissolve the bad energy in these areas. They should be left burning for a minimum of 3 hours a day.

The chi that enters your home may not be beneficial, as it will have been affected by its journey.

Make a mixture of sea salt in warm water to sprinkle at the entrance to your home to purify the chi as it enters.

Good *chi* should
be encouraged to enter
your home.

Chandeliers or other light fixtures with hanging crystals placed just inside or outside the home encourage good chi to enter.

CHAPTER FIVE

Dealing with Environmental Hazards

Few of us are lucky enough to have so much land that we do not have to deal with the effect of nearby buildings or structures. Although most of these will make little difference, all schools of feng shui believe that certain elements of nearby structures, known as poison arrows, can create negative power, known as shar chi, or killing breath. If your house is hit by the effect of such poison arrows it will have an extremely malignant effect on the luck of everyone who lives in the building.

It is one of the basic principles of feng shui that you should check for poison arrows outside and defend against them before you make any effort to create good feng shui inside. Luckily such elements are quite easy to spot, once you know what you are looking for, and the techniques for dealing with them are fairly simple. As well as established environmental hazards such as power lines or pollution, anything sharp that points towards your home—particularly at the front door—is suspect.

There are three main ways to proceed when dealing with poison arrows: create structures to block or deflect the shar chi; introduce barriers to dissolve it; or place a hostile structure to counter it.

If the sharp corner of a neighboring building points towards your house, particularly at the front door, it is a poison arrow sending negative energy towards you. Deflect the harmful shar chi with a mirror above the door.

A road leading directly towards
your home is bad feng shui, but
planting a clump of bushy plants will
absorb the negative energy
coming towards you.

The approach to your house should be gentle and curved—straight driveways or paths should be rerouted.

Harmful energy can also be absorbed by installing a bright light between your home and the poison arrow.

A tree or post directly in front of the
front door will prevent positive chi from entering.
Hang a metal wind chime outside, or install a
bright light to deal with the problem.

Houses near places with too much
YIN energy, such as churches, hospitals,
or prisons, will be adversely affected. Make
sure your home is full of YANG energy by
filling it with BRIGHT LIGHTS,
MUSIC, and VIBRANT COLORS.

*If there is a high wall or tall building
in front of your home, install a bright light at your
front entrance and keep it switched on.*

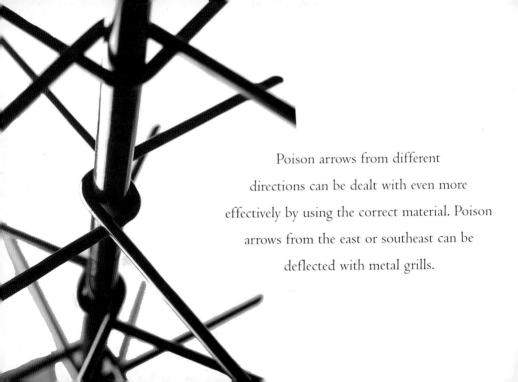

Poison arrows from different directions can be dealt with even more effectively by using the correct material. Poison arrows from the east or southeast can be deflected with metal grills.

Poison arrows from
the **northeast** or
southwest can be
deflected with hedges.

Poison arrows from
the north can be
blocked by a wall, and
from the south by a
wall with water
running down it.

Safeguard the west
and northwest with a
wall painted red.

CHAPTER SIX

The Concept of Sacred Space

Sacred places have existed in every culture around the world from early civilization. Some are natural—mountains, hidden caves, and shady glens—others are man-made like Stonehenge and Chichen Itza. They usually take advantage of naturally-occurring energy lines and represent places on earth where the energy vibration is higher than normal. Especially powerful spots are usually reserved for ceremonial use, as their energies are too powerful for everyday living.

In the home, it is important for your emotional well-being to create your own sacred space where you can relax. A room with powerful yin energy is an ideal setting for meditation and inner reflection, a place where you can examine and replenish your inner resources. As you become calm, strong healing energies can be accessed and you can contact the very core of your being—who we are at a spiritual level.

A sacred space does not need to be a large area. A quiet corner can be just as successful as an empty room. Make time to use your sacred space regularly, but do not remain in an area of strong yin energy for too long, or you may become lethargic, and lacking in energy or motivation.

Your sacred SPACE can be anywhere you are likely
to have some PRIVACY on a regular basis at some point
during the day. Make it clear to the rest of the family
that you do not want to be disturbed—or arrange some
TIME ALONE in the house.

If it is evening, turn off the lights and
burn candles to relax your eyes and your spirits.
Burn lavender incense to relax.

Listen to some *tranquil music*, watch a favorite video, or *read* a book.

*Or sit in peace
and enjoy the luxury
of some time set aside
just for you.*

People who have a pet are less depressed
and anxious and recover from illnesses quicker
than those who don't. Pets also offer the opportunity
for an undemanding play or a cuddle. Stroking
a cat has been shown to bring relaxation and a
drop in stress levels.

Bathing can be a relaxing experience if you are not rushing to get ready to go out.

*Make sure you have enough time
to lie back and enjoy the warm water,
put fresh towels to warm, and light
the bathroom with candles.*

127

Add a few drops of jasmine oil
to the water. Lie back and let those
negative feelings drift away.

> *"Inside myself is a place where
> I live all alone, and that's where you renew
> your springs that never dry up."*
>
> PEARL S. BUCK

If you find that instead of relaxing you are sitting worrying, make a list of everything that is concerning you. When problems are written down on paper they often do not look so bad, but put the paper aside for half an hour and resolve to deal with the issues later.

If you feel stress building up at work,
sit down, breathe deeply, and take a five-minute break.
You will get through your tasks much quicker when you
come back to them refreshed.

If your bedroom is used as your sacred space, make sure it is relaxing and full of yin energy. Color schemes should be muted and the lighting dimmed

Do not have mirrors reflecting
the bed in your bedroom, or
a television. They will bring
you disturbed sleep and bad
relationship luck.

CHAPTER SEVEN

Feng Shui in the Garden

The natural environment around your home is just as important as the building itself. Good chi is assured when your garden is growing well with lush plants—healthy plants are a potent indication of good feng shui. The placement of important elements such as water features and trees, how paths move around the space, and the colors of the plants in different areas should all be considered, as they can affect the flow of chi into the home, thus bringing good or bad luck.

You must also consider yin and yang, and the five elements—fire, metal, earth, wood, and water—to ensure that everything is balanced and harmonious. Selecting auspicious plants for each sector of the garden will also enhance good chi. However small or large your garden is, its feng shui can be improved with a little planning. Never treat the garden in isolation, it must be planned in conjunction with the location and orientation of the house itself. The position of water in relation to the building is very important, as correctly placed it brings wealth and generates auspicious chi, but badly placed it will cause these to flow away. If you introduce any large structures into the garden, be sure they do not create poison arrows or block the flow of chi toward the front door.

137

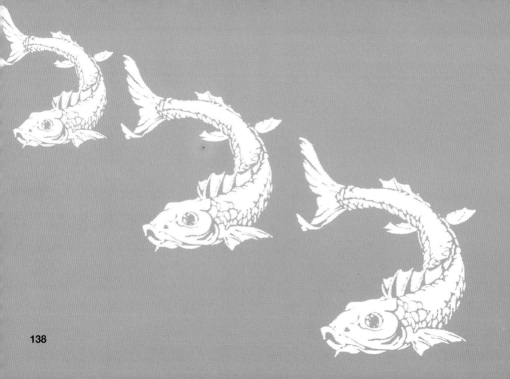

THE NORTH FACING GARDEN

The element of the north is water, so features such as a pond are very auspicious. However, make sure that the water is moving or aerated—keeping fish creates excellent yang energy. Do not place the pond to the right of the front door—when standing at the entrance looking out—as this can encourage the man of the house to stray in his affections.

THE SOUTH FACING GARDEN

The element of the south is fire,
and as fire is the symbol of warmth,
plants will thrive here. Make sure the
garden is well lit.

THE WEST OR NORTHWEST FACING GARDEN

These two directions are associated with the element of metal, so features such as a metal wind chimes are very auspicious. However, make sure that you do not hang them from a tree as the elements of metal and wood clash. Earth elements such as rocks and stones are also good in this area.

THE EAST OR SOUTHEAST FACING GARDEN

The element of these two directions is wood,

so ornamental trees and plants are good features—

particularly magnolia and peonies.

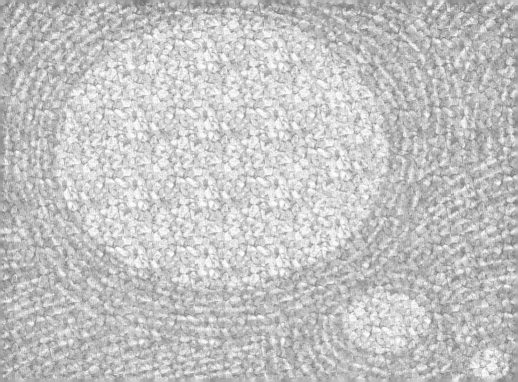

THE NORTHEAST OR SOUTHWEST FACING GARDEN

The element of both these directions is earth, so rocks, paving-slab paths, and designs of pebbles are all suitable. An oriental garden of raked gravel would be a particularly good feature here.

If your garden is on a rooftop,
do not include any water features—water high up
symbolizes great danger and will bring
misfortune to the household.

Yellow chrysanthemums
are auspicious and attract
good feng shui to
the garden.

Plum blossom symbolizes longevity
and good fortune, but for the best effect it should
be planted in the back garden.

A single magnolia tree in the front garden will attract great contentment, while at the back it symbolizes the collection of great wealth.

*The lily is particularly auspicious
and brings good feng shui throughout the year.*

Lotus blossoms bring
peace *and* contentment.

Bulbs such as narcissus
bring great fortune.

Keep cactus and plants with *thorns* or *spiked leaves* away from the house as they can direct **negative energy** towards the home.

Bamboo is a very powerful
antidote to bad feng shui and
it is also an ancient
symbol of longevity.

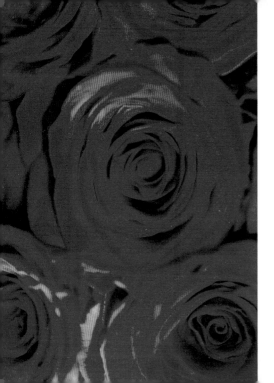

RED FLOWERS bring good luck wherever they are grown, but are particularly auspicious in the south. YELLOW FLOWERS are best in the southwest and northeast. ORANGE FLOWERS do well in all these areas.

In the north grow bluebells and purple flowers—particularly if this is behind the home. White flowers also do well in the north and northwest, as white symbolizes metal.

CHAPTER EIGHT

Using Color

Color plays an important part in every aspect of our lives. It surrounds us almost everywhere we go, but we may not always be fully conscious of the effect it has. Becoming more aware of colors and finding them in unexpected places will enrich your life. When you understand the relationship between certain colors and how they affect you, you will also understand a great deal about yourself. Colors have definite symbolism for individual people and the use of color therapy to treat both mental and physical ailments is growing.

Every color has a positive or negative effect, depending on where it is or who is wearing it. Everyone has favorite colors, but not everyone understands how colors can affect the way you feel and the way others look at you. Wearing carefully chosen colors can give you the power to control the way people respond to you, and decorating with the right colors can soothe your mood or stimulate creativity. Adding or removing even just a tiny amount of color can alter the whole mood of a room or outfit. Color can either enhance your sense of well-being or conflict with it to cause a feeling of disturbance. Being creative with color will awaken your imagination and expand your sense of being.

RED

Red is a very strong color and used with care
it will boost your emotional energy. Do not use
too much red as it can be overpowering.

ORANGE

Orange is stimulating, but much
gentler than red.

YELLOW

This is another strong color that can be overpowering
in large quantities. Used carefully, it heightens your energy and
makes you feel warm and happy.

GREEN

Green is the most restful on the eye of all
the colors—it is everywhere in nature. It will
bring a feeling of peace.

BLUE

The color blue can be rather cold, and
bring out feelings of fear and insecurity. Warmer
shades are more relaxing and peaceful.

VIOLET

This is a mixture of red and blue and comes
in a variety of shades from lavender to purple. Too much
of it can be unsettling, but used with restraint
it is stimulating.

MAGENTA

A cool red that contains some blue,
magenta is sensuous and exciting, but too
much can be oppressive.

CYAN

This is a mixture of green and blue
and is a gentle and peaceful color that will
bring happiness and relaxation.

A successful color scheme needs both contrast and harmony. Contrast brings life, drama, and excitement to the room, harmony makes the room work as a living space.

When introducing contrast, use **light** and **dark**, **rough** and **smooth**. Choose colors that are **opposite** each other, such as blue and orange, red and green, and yellow and violet, but make sure one is **stronger** than the other, as using **equal** amounts will cause them to clash.

*To introduce harmony, make sure there
is one dominant tone that runs through the
scheme, giving different areas of the room
something in common.*

Most people dress in their favorite colors, but you can use color to alter how people see you. Dramatic colors can make you stand out and look bold and alive, muted colors make less of a statement, but give a calm impression.

Personal preference plays a big part—if you do not feel comfortable wearing BRIGHT COLORS, then they will not work for you. However you could dress mainly in more MUTED TONES but accessorize in bright colors.

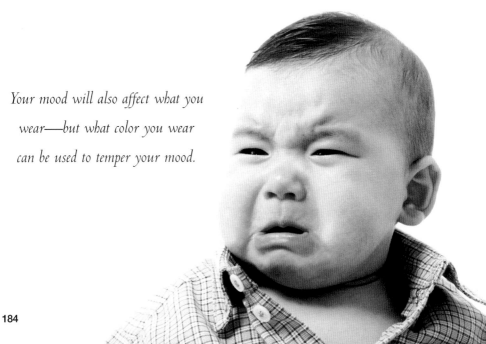

Your mood will also affect what you wear—but what color you wear can be used to temper your mood.

*If you feel anxious or angry, dress
in muted* neutral *colors, such as*
cream, gray, *or paler-toned*
greens *and* blues.

If you feel unhappy
or lacking in energy, dress in
reds, oranges, or yellows to
lift your spirits.

If you feel stressed,
dress in pale green,
cyan, or greeny-blues
to calm yourself down.

CHAPTER NINE

The Natural Home

Using natural materials in the home will bring it in tune with nature and create an important link between the human environment and the natural world. The beautiful grain and subtle luster of timber stimulates the senses and has a timeless appeal, while scented woods such as cedar or sandalwood impart a delicate fragrance to the whole room. Other natural materials that are widely used in interiors include ceramics and metal. As well as being beautiful in their own right, they also bring the earth and metal elements of feng shui into the home, and they can be placed in the appropriate sector to energize it. Natural elements work best when used in simple ways. Each element should also be as close as possible to its original state—unpainted wood, unglazed ceramics, and unpolished metal are better than over-worked finishes that no longer look "natural."

Modern equipment, such as television and computers, generate electromagnetic fields that are bad for the health, but these can be countered using very simple techniques, as plants are excellent for absorbing any chemical pollutants in the atmosphere. All paints or cleaning products used should have natural ingredients and as few chemicals as possible to avoid polluting your environment.

190

Natural wood appeals to the senses. Choose wood with beautiful grain and a natural or waxed finish, so its beauty shines through. Scented woods, such as sandalwood or cedar wood, used in items for clothing storage both give a delicate fragrance and deter insects.

Natural colors and *simple*
finishes are both *subtle*
and easy to clean.

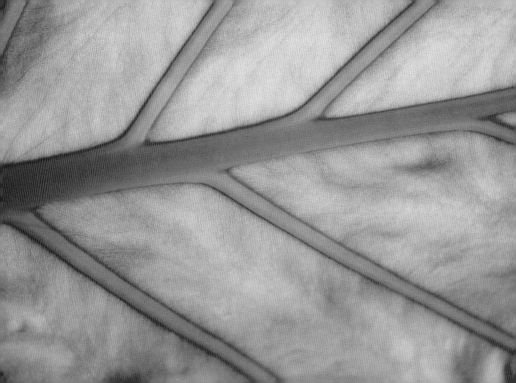

Plants in the home will absorb
harmful chemicals. Azaleas, rubber plants, and
bamboo palms all remove formaldehyde.

Natural crystals are excellent
feng shui energizers. For maximum benefit,
place a bowl of crystals in the earth sectors
of southwest or northeast.

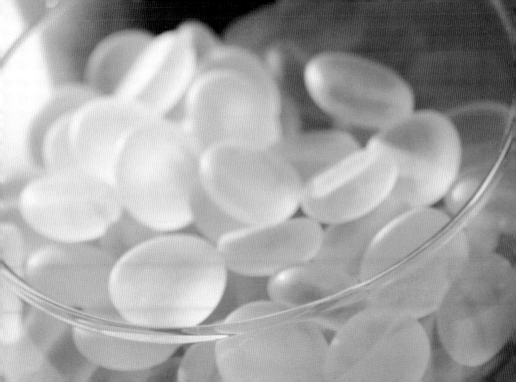

Try not to introduce chemicals into your
home environment and take steps to reduce the
build-up of pollutants that will affect your well-being.
Choose cleaning materials with a high proportion
of natural ingredients.

Choose wool, cotton, or natural-fiber rugs
laid on a wood, cork, or ceramic floor, rather than
wall-to-wall synthetic carpets.

Oranges have a refreshing scent that revives the spirits. Make your own potpourri by mixing dried peel from an organic orange, wood shavings, and dried chilies, and adding a few drops of orange essential oil.

Plants give off oxygen *to* enhance *the atmosphere and remove carbon dioxide. Humans breathe* oxygen *and give off carbon dioxide—so plants in the home are* beneficial *to both.*

First impressions are lasting impressions.
Greet the visitor to your home with an inspiring flower
arrangement that will spread positive energy from the
entrance throughout the building.

CHAPTER TEN

Making Space

With the needs and stresses of everyday living and family life, we sometimes forget about making space in the day for ourselves. Everyone needs some time to be themselves and do just want they want to do, but often it is far too easy to go along with what everyone else wants. Making time for yourself is not selfish—it is just as essential as eating and drinking to keep you fit and healthy. Just a few minutes a day can make all the difference. Once you get into the habit you will find it much easier to recognize slices of time when they become available.

As well as space in your day, you need to find space in your home. If your lifestyle no longer seems to work in the way it should, look at your surroundings and decide if you are using them in the most efficient way. Most people use their houses in conventional set ways, but there is no need to do so if another way will work better for you. Rearranging the space and moving people or functions into different rooms can sometimes free up whole areas that you did not even realize you had! The key is learning how to look objectively at the way you use your home and to be realistic about your needs, and about those of other family members.

If you never have enough time and
start the day already feeling stressed...

...get up half an hour earlier
to give yourself time to get ready
without having to rush around.

When you are really busy it is difficult to find time for yourself.

Begin putting aside at least five minutes each day
in which you consciously relax and do nothing.

Nobody can be perfect at everything.

Pick what is most important to you and concentrate on doing your best in those areas.

"If I keep a green bough in my heart,
the singing bird will come."

CHINESE PROVERB

*Make an effort to keep
in touch with old friends.*

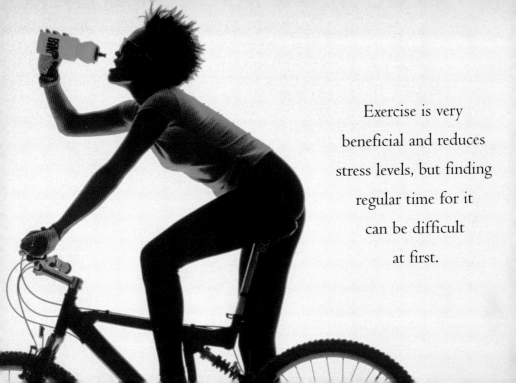

Exercise is very
beneficial and reduces
stress levels, but finding
regular time for it
can be difficult
at first.

Instead of eating lunch at your desk,
make time for a ten-minute walk outside. The
fresh air and exercise will increase your energy
levels to help you cope with the afternoon.

Get a good night's sleep.

Z Z Z Z Z Z Z z z

If you have problems getting to sleep, add a few drops of lavender oil to your evening bath, or on a tissue near your pillow.

A *stressed* body leads to
a *stressed* mind.

Cut down on stimulants
such as coffee, tea, alcohol,
and nicotine. Drink
lots of water.

You are not SUPERHUMAN—you
can only do what you can do.

Learn to say
"No."

Make one room in the house a place where you
can relax, or do your own creative work.

Take a realistic look at how you are using available space. *If you always eat in the kitchen, use the dining room for something else.*

As children grow, they seem to take over the whole house.

However important your children are in your life,
you need space for yourself as well to be a good parent.
Give the children the biggest bedrooms, and make it clear that
all their things should be kept inside. The living room
can then become your sanctuary.

There really is no spare room in the house.

You do not need a whole room—a comfortable corner where you will not be disturbed for a reasonable amount of time is sufficient.

PART TWO

Harmonizing Mind, Body, and Spirit

CHAPTER ELEVEN

Understanding Your Aur

The human aura is a rainbow play of color that extends in an oval shape around your entire body up to a distance of around three feet. It consists of several layers with different colors and it draws and absorbs the life force from the atmosphere. Your aura is very sensitive to your health, moods, and emotions—if everything is fine the colors will be pure, harmonious, and luminous, but if you have either a physical or emotional problem, part of it will become muddy and darker. Which part of it is affected and how dark and dirty the colors become depends on what is wrong, and how serious it is. Sometimes the shape and size of the aura are also affected, or the pattern may change.

Some people are sensitive enough to see the aura of those around them and they can tell just by looking at it if anything is wrong, and what the problem is. Healers can help you heal yourself—but only with your cooperation. It is also quite usual for a healer to be able to see problems in the aura well before they manifest themselves in physical or emotional problems, because weaknesses can be present before an illness takes hold. In these cases, the healer can help you take steps to prevent the illness from developing.

AURA COLORS:

Gold

Great intellect and higher spiritual development

AURA COLORS:

White

Purity and spiritual development

AURA COLORS:
Red
Vibrant personality and sexuality

Orange

Life-force energy and joyousness

Yellow

Astral body and ability to interact with the world

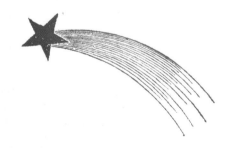

Greens & Blues

Health and personality

Violet & Purple

Psychic evolvement, higher self, and spirituality

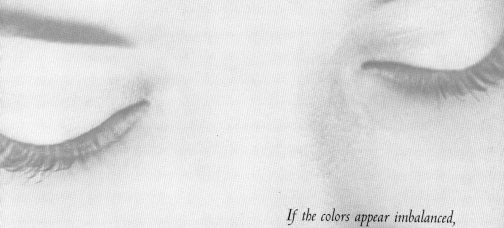

If the colors appear imbalanced,
it is an indication of dysfunction in the
relevant area. Gray and murky colors
indicate ill health and depression.

The chakras are the energy centers of the body—the word comes from the Sanskrit word for "wheel." If they are out of balance, a color healing practitioner can apply therapy to correct the problem.

Although there are many different schools of thought, it is generally recognized that there are several chakras.

CHAKRA COLORS:

Red

The first chakra is located at the
base of the spine, and relates to the
body. It represents our connection to
the earth and provides the sexual
energy to reproduce.

CHAKRA COLORS:

Orange

The second chakra is located

halfway between the spine and the

navel, in the belly area. It represents

desires and passions and is the source

of creative energy.

CHAKRA COLORS:

Yellow

The third chakra is located at the solar

plexus, just above the navel. It

represents our connection to the world

around us and provides personal power

and the energy to take action.

CHAKRA COLORS:

Green

The fourth chakra is located centrally in the body, level with the heart. It represents romantic and sexual love and is the source of compassion, understanding, and the ability to develop relationships with others.

CHAKRA COLORS:

Blue

The fifth chakra is located at

the throat. It represents communication,

both how we communicate with

others and how our body

communicates with itself.

CHAKRA COLORS:

Indigo

The sixth chakra is located above and between the eyes, and is sometimes known as the third eye. It represents deep understanding and insight, and provides an increased level of awareness and access to inner wisdom.

CHAKRA COLORS:

Violet

The seventh chakra is located at
the top of the head. It is the source
of our thoughts, beliefs, and dreams
and represents the intersection
of mind and body.

Color therapists can identify which
CHAKRA is imbalanced and can use LIGHT and COLOR
to BALANCE and HARMONIZE the body, which
stabilizes both physical and emotional states.

CHAPTER TWELVE

Clearing the Mind

Every day our minds are filled with a continuous flow of jumbled ideas, thoughts, and emotions—even more so if we are anxious, angry, guilty, or unhappy. By instinct, we tend to feel that if we keep thinking about a problem we will eventually arrive at a practical solution. In reality, it may be impossible to resolve conflicts, which makes us feel even more stressed and anxious. While the mind overworks, the body is underactive and so tends to sink into lethargy, paralyzed by the amount that needs to be accomplished.

If you can learn to empty your mind of unwanted thoughts and worries, you will become much calmer and will be able to observe what passes through your mind without inner judgement or comment. You will become detached from the rush of the outside world, but at the same time more aware of the detail of life around you. As you become more practiced at discarding unwanted mind matter, you will become more concentrated and focused and able to approach life in a different way. Clearing the mind leads to a healthier body, as it no longer has to cope with the rush of adrenaline with no physical action. Techniques for mind clearing are easy to learn—they just need practice and commitment.

If you have a problem, try and talk
it through with someone. If the problem is being caused
by someone in your life, the sooner it can be discussed
and resolved between you, the less chance it has
to build up resentment and anger.

There is no point in worrying about what might happen. Most of the things we worry about never do happen—take action on something you can change instead.

When you feel STRESS building up, take several
deep breaths and try to empty your mind. It can be
surprisingly difficult to do, but persevere until you acquire
the ability to step away from your worries
for a brief period.

Do not allow *angry* or *guilty* thoughts to fester in your mind. If you can take action to resolve them, do so. If there is nothing you can do, *learn to let them go.*

RELAXATION TECHNIQUE:

Sit in a comfortable chair or lie on a bed. Close your
eyes and concentrate on breathing slowly and evenly. Starting
with your toes, clench and then relax each muscle, moving slowly
up your body. At the end of the exercise, lie quietly and
visualize a beautiful natural scene for a few moments.
Open your eyes, but stay still until you
feel ready to move.

Combat *negative* thoughts by continually making *positive* statements about yourself and others.

We are responsible only for our own

ATTITUDES and BEHAVIOR.

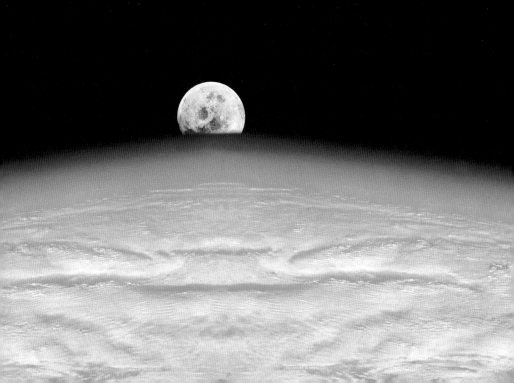

Change what you can change,
accept what you cannot change.

Learn to forgive yourself.

273

CHAPTER THIRTEEN

The Breath of Life

The process of breathing is more than just taking in oxygen and expelling carbon dioxide from the body. Everyone knows how to breathe—it is a process so natural that we can forget we are doing it, but if we stop breathing we will die. Many Buddhist traditions use the act of breathing as a focus for meditation. It may sound easy, but concentrating on breathing in and out regularly without being distracted by every passing thought can be immensely difficult—it can take months or even years to get it right.

Most of us breathe far too shallowly, failing to use the full capacity of our lungs. Breathing correctly is the "breath of life," and it will increase your energy, reduce stress, and help you sleep better. Deep, unforced breathing is achieved when the diaphragm and chest muscles work together in harmony, and it can give you a new feeling about yourself. Correct breathing also aids correct posture—the two work together in perfect harmony as the body comes into alignment with itself. Deep breaths increase the amount of oxygen in the body, which eases tension, prevents back stress, and improves circulation. If you work at it, in time deeper breathing will become as natural as shallow breathing once was.

"Our breath is the bridge from our body to our mind."

Thich Nhat Hanh—*The Miracle of Mindfulness*

Begin by getting into a
comfortable position, but
keep your back straight and
your spine extended.

Breathe in deeply and slowly, and without pausing breathe out again as deeply.

Count as you breathe; one as you breathe in,

two as you breathe out, and so on.

Try to focus on breathing to the exclusion of
all else until you have reached the count of ten.

1   2   3   4   5   6

1   2   3   4   5   6   7

If thoughts intrude and you forget
to count, start again at one.

8   9   10

8   9   10

Gradually you will be able to just sit still in the present, concentrating only on your breathing, for increasing periods of time.

"Breath will cut through thinking because you have to let go to breathe."

Jakusho Kwong—*Zen in America*

When you are *stressed*, your breathing becomes shallower and faster, making the blood more acidic and leading to *hyperventilation* and *panic*.

Taking two or three DEEP BREATHS can lift you above the stress and relieve anxiety quickly.

If you breathe using your upper chest,
you will never use the full capacity of your lungs.

Sit in a chair with arms in front of a mirror. Breathe in deeply and see if your shoulders rise—if they do, you are an upper-chest breather.

To correct upper-chest breathing, sit with your arms on the chair armrests and push down with your forearms and elbows as you inhale— this will prevent you from using the wrong muscles.

Repeat the exercise ten times, exhaling for six to eight seconds, and inhaling for two to three seconds.

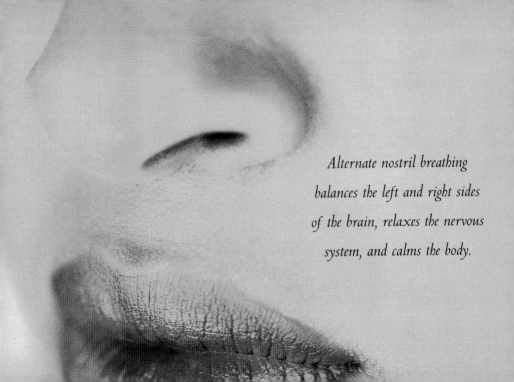

Alternate nostril breathing balances the left and right sides of the brain, relaxes the nervous system, and calms the body.

Sit straight, but relaxed, with one hand to your face, so you can use the thumb to block one nostril and a finger to block the other. Close your right nostril and breathe in to the count of three, then close the left and exhale to the count of six through the right nostril. Breathe in through the right, and continue alternately for 10 rounds.

Britain and Central Europe

CHAPTER FOURTEEN

Life Coaching

Many people know where they want to be, but cannot work out how to get there. A professional life coach helps you achieve your ambitions in both work and personal life—they act as an advisor and as a sounding board for ideas. While a therapist may look at how your past is affecting you, a life coach will focus on building strengths and learning strategies for change. However, consultation can be expensive and you can be your own life coach by following a few simple steps.

Identifying and understanding what is blocking your progress is the key to moving forward. Looking back at your life, you must learn to focus on achievements and not failures. Simply looking at your past and present in a different way can change how you think about yourself and give you more confidence in the future. Realizing what you have achieved will also focus your mind on what you really value and want in life—which will reveal which direction you need to move in to achieve your ambitions. Once you have established where you are going, you can focus on activities that feed this vision and move away from those that do not. There is no need to think big—even quite small changes can make a big difference if they are part of a concerted plan.

293

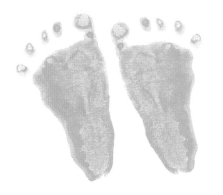

Take steps to achieve success in your life.

Make a list of your three greatest achievements,
your three greatest failures, and the three most important
lessons you have learned in life. Your final list
will tell you what is important to you and
what you really want.

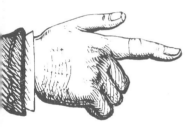

Be specific

If you want a better social life,
decide on how social you want it to be.
Do you want just the odd evening out,
or to be out every night? If you want
more money, are you talking about a
few hundred dollars or a few million?

Be your own best friend.

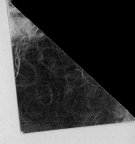

Never talk yourself down—tell yourself
how well you are doing, enjoy your own
company, be positive.

See yourself as others see you.

Ask your trusted friends what they like—or dislike—about you. The results will almost certainly surprise you and make you reevaluate how you present yourself to others.

Ask yourself what
you are afraid of.

If a big leap in a new
direction is too scary,
take small steps—
you will be there before
you know it.

Feed the vision.

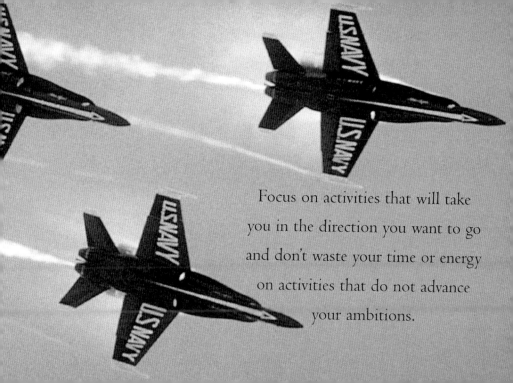

Focus on activities that will take
you in the direction you want to go
and don't waste your time or energy
on activities that do not advance
your ambitions.

Live for yourself.

It's your life—don't spend time trying to be
what others think you should be if you know it is not
going to make you happy.

Be open to new
experiences.

Even if you think you will not like it,
don't dismiss any possibilities until you have
thought them through properly.

Be accountable.

Blaming other people for our mistakes is disempowering. We cannot choose how others behave toward us, but we can choose how we will react.

Identify the energy drains on your life.

Everyone has things that make them feel negative about life and that we tend to avoid doing. Make a list and start checking them off.

Focus 100% on
what you are doing.

Feeling that you should be doing something else saps your concentration on the task in hand. PRIORITIZE your workload and stick to what is really IMPORTANT. Resolve to spend a set amount of time entirely FOCUSED on your current project, then take a short break to answer other urgent queries.

Be financially disciplined.

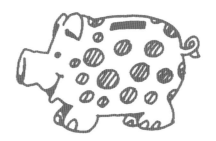

Nothing stops us from doing what we want more than the lack of money. Make a financial plan to clear any debts as quickly as you can. Check interest rates on credit cards and cut up the most expensive. Make a list of monthly expenditures so you know exactly where the money is going, then try to cut expenses by at least 15%. Try to put a little aside each month as a fighting fund to enable you to achieve your dream.

Don't forget your family.

Your career is not everything—remember your family and friends and leave some time in your life for them.

CHAPTER THIRTEEN

Love or Fear

As we pass through life, we can either spend our time on earth enjoying love or in fearfulness. It is impossible not to feel fear sometimes, but some people live their whole lives subject to it. No one likes to be afraid, so we spend our lives avoiding scary situations—which just makes things worse. The way to vanquish fear is to face up to it—and in many cases, what we are afraid of turns out not to be as bad as expected. The power of imagination has blown things out of proportion and made things much worse than they really are. Refusing to face your fears often results in the development of phobias, but facing your fears can lessen their grip and even vanquish them.

Love can be a much more positive emotion—love for yourself, for your family, and for other people around you. Love helps you achieve unity with those who are in the world with you. Love creates healthy interdependence and teaches us to be more tolerant of other people's differences. Whereas fear narrows your horizons, love opens them up and allows you to become more receptive to the world.

We all have the power to choose—love or fear, open or closed, light or dark—you just have to take that first step along the correct path.

"There's nothing wrong with fear except fear itself."

President Roosevelt

A certain amount of **fear** *is natural—it stops us from taking silly risks in life. It is when fear prevents you from living life as you would choose that it becomes unnatural.*

Chronic fear causes all kinds of physical problems from loss of appetite and nausea, to nervous habits and chest pains.

Fear can mentally paralyze, so that you are unable to make reasonable and balanced decisions. As it grows, fear becomes self-perpetuating and the very thing you fear may develop because of the way you are reacting to what happens to you.

Feel the fear—
and do it anyway.

Facing up to your fears is the best way to vanquish them. The dread of the unknown is almost always much worse than actually coping with the situation you are afraid of. The very act of taking action gives you something to concentrate on, leaving little room for fear to build up in your mind.

Keep things in perspective.

Look at what you are frightened of, imagine the worst possible outcome and decide what you would do if it happened. Once you have thought it through, and have strategies in place to cope, any other outcome must be an improvement.

Love yourself.

If you LOVE yourself and consider yourself to be a worthwhile person, others will LOVE you too. Forgive your own mistakes—everybody makes them.

Appreciating that your own true value *has nothing to do with vanity or pride, it is just being* honest *with yourself.*

Look at yourself objectively and make
a list of all your good points, and another of your bad
points. If you are particularly critical, the second list
will be longer, but study it and decide what you would
like to change, and then set about doing it.

Love is the most powerful energy we have;
it helps us heal ourselves and others.

Love contains forgiveness, compassion, generosity, kindness, and caring for yourself and for others.

"All you need is love."

John Lennon

338

Without love, you will never be able to experience true joy. Love is a precious emotion that should be shared whenever possible.

If your LIFE is full of LOVE, there is no room left for fear.

CHAPTER SIXTEEN

Coping with Stress

If they are honest, most people would say that they would like a less stressful life, yet at the same time they may feel it is impossible to make the necessary changes to achieve it. Caught between the demands of career and family, it can be difficult to see a positive way forward, and the nature of stress itself can make it hard to be objective.

A little stress at the right time can sometimes be beneficial, pushing us into action when it is needed, but too much is paralyzing and prevents us from working at maximum capacity. Overstressed people generally have little energy, find it difficult to sleep and suffer from a variety of health problems. Whatever triggers the stress, the body's physical reaction tends to be the same. Heart and pulse rate increases, adrenal glands become active, and we become strained and anxious mentally.

You can learn to cope with stress by following a few simple steps—some of which are designed to stop the stress building up in the first place, and others that will help you cope with it. The demands of modern life make it impossible to avoid stressful situations completely, but you can learn to get your life back under control, and begin to enjoy it again.

Emotional Symptom
of Stress:

Anxiety

Shyness

Depression

Difficulty concentrating

Loneliness

Irritability

Indecisiveness

Thoughts of death or suicide

Feeling worthless or guilty

Physical Symptoms of Stress:

Breathing problems

Constipation

Digestive problems

Dizziness

Tiredness

Frequent illness

Crying easily

Headaches

Blood pressure problems

Stress-inducing Events:

Death of a close relative

Divorce or separation

Marriage

Pregnancy and birth

Retirement

Moving home

Change in financial circumstances

Major changes at work

Christmas or other major holidays

Vacations

Take physical exercise

Taking adequate physical exercise is the single most beneficial action you can take to reduce stress levels. You need to take a brisk walk—or similar exercise—at least 5 days a week.

Adjust your diet.

Eat a wide variety of real food, avoiding
fast food and processed foods. Have at least five
helpings of fresh vegetables each day.

Relax

Learn to switch off and relax at least once a day for a minimum of 30 minutes.

Sleep

Everyone needs at least six hours of SLEEP a night. Too much SLEEP is as bad as too little. Use relaxation techniques and deep breathing to help you drop off to SLEEP easier and faster.

Laugh

Laughter not only makes you feel better, it is also good exercise. Try to find something to laugh about at least once a day.

Let go

Nobody is perfect. You can only do what
you can do, but if you keep on doing it you will
get there in the end.

CHAPTER SEVENTEEN

Meditation

Zen Buddhists believe that mental peace and clarity is achieved through meditation. Basic meditation involves sitting silently and allowing the mind to empty of all thoughts, so that your own, innate wisdom comes to the surface. Like many such simple-sounding processes, it is often very difficult to achieve success without a great deal of practice. When you try it for the first time, the constant activity of your mind will be impossible to still, with stray thoughts constantly interrupting all attempts to focus on one specific thing.

Meditation is the key to serenity and there are techniques that will help you in your search. Different techniques work for different people, so if a particular scenario does not work, try another until you find one that does. Finally, however, practice is the key. If you want to meditate successfully you must set aside some time every day. It does not have to be a very long period—just a few minutes each day is an excellent start. It is better in a small amount of time that you can manage regularly, rather than a longer period that will be difficult to fit into your daily schedule. As you begin to feel the benefits in your life, meditation will take on a momentum of its own and you will undoubtedly manage to find more time.

"For penetrating to the depths of one's own true self-nature and for attaining a vitality valid on all occasions, nothing can surpass meditation in the midst of activity."

Master Hakuin, 1685-1768

You will need somewhere quiet and peaceful to meditate. Choose somewhere comfortable, where you will not be disturbed. Try and use the same place each day so your surroundings will become associated with the act of meditation.

Lighting should be average—dark places are not suitable—
and the temperature should be adequate to enable you to
sit still for some time.

Try to meditate *at the same time each day, every day. Get into a comfortable position, either sitting or lying down, that you will be able to maintain for some time. Rest your hands loosely in your lap.*

If you are meditating with a group of people, wear dark or neutral clothing to avoid distracting them.

Some people like to sound a bell or burn incense as they prepare to meditate. Rituals like this can soon begin to act as a trigger, getting you in the correct frame of mind.

To begin with, 15-20 minutes will be enough, but you can build up to longer periods over time.

Keep your eyes downcast, looking forward. Some people like to close their eyes, but this may lead you to fall asleep.

Allow your mouth to relax,
but keep your lips together with
your tongue resting on the roof
of your mouth. Keep your
spine straight and center
your balance.

Take a few deep breaths, exhaling fully, then allow your breath to settle into its natural rhythm.

Focus your attention by counting breaths in and out, but do not try to control your breathing or count aloud. Count up to ten and then start again at one.

If you find thoughts have intruded and you have lost count, begin again at one. It may take some practice before you can concentrate only on your breathing, but you will soon be able to meditate for longer periods.

CHAPTER EIGHTEEN

Healthy Eating

If we eat low quality or the wrong kind of food, it lowers our vitality and can lead to ill health, both mentally and physically. Most Westerners eat far too much fatty or rich foods, which clog up our systems and prevent fluids from moving around the body easily. This not only results in obesity, but can also lead to a host of other symptoms such as bloating, bowel disorders, aching joints, lack of concentration, depression, and tiredness. Balance in our diet is important. A healthy diet contains a small proportion of rich foods, along with vegetables, fruit, grains, and carbohydrates. Cutting out any part completely will inevitably lead to problems.

An important part of eating correctly is to enjoy your food. No matter how much good it is doing you physically, unless you also enjoy it mentally then you will not gain the best possible nourishment from it. Including a variety of different tastes and textures in our diet makes food more interesting, and a few "treats" occasionally will lift the spirits without doing too much harm.

Your new, healthy diet will increase your energy and clear your mind and body. If you are committed, it takes only one month to change the habits of a lifetime, so your new eating habits will soon be part of your everyday lifestyle.

The modern diet contains a large amount of rich foods,
but these are difficult for our bodies to process in large quantities.
Our ancestors ate far more vegetables, grains, and carbohydrates, and
their diet was healthier. The ideal proportion of rich foods to
other types is shown on the chart to the right.

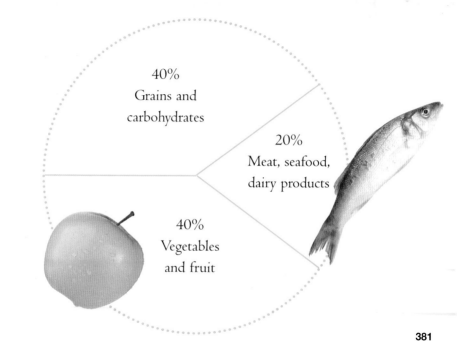

40%
Grains and
carbohydrates

20%
Meat, seafood,
dairy products

40%
Vegetables
and fruit

When we eat food that is not healthy, our bodies react.

Some common responses include:

Bloating after eating

Lack of concentration

Aching joints

Headaches

Indigestion

Wind

Stomach pains

Excess mucus

Any food that you crave or have an extreme dislike to is possibly something you are sensitive to. Try and eliminate it from your diet for a few weeks and see what effect this has on your health.

Some substitutes for everyday foods:

MILK—Soya, oat, or rice milk

CHEESE—Goat's or sheep's milk cheese

ORANGE JUICE—Apple, pear,
or grape juice

TEA—Herbal teas

SUGARY FOODS—Switch to foods
naturally sweetened with
fruit juice or molasses

COFFEE—Carob coffee or chicory

ALCOHOL—low alcohol beer, organic beer, and wine

WHEAT—rice, oats, and products made from other grains

WHEAT BISCUITS—oat biscuits or rice cakes

WHEAT BREAD—rye bread or pumpernickel bread

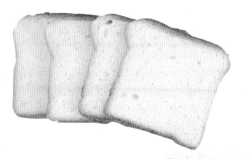

Eat good quality food—home-grown or organic foods are best, as commercially grown crops are heavily sprayed with pesticides, while farm-reared animals are routinely treated with hormones and antibiotics.

If you cannot eat organic, avoid root vegetables such as carrots. Leafy vegetables are less contaminated, but eat the outer leaves rather than the heart. The outer leaves also contain the most vitamins and minerals.

Make your food look attractive on the plate, and allow yourself regular treats as you change your diet to healthier foods.

Eat regularly—when you eat at *regular* intervals you will start to feel hungry at those times of the day. This also means that your *energy* levels will be replenished at intervals throughout the day.

Avoid eating late at night and allow time—at least half an hour—after meals to sit down and digest your food properly.

Eat only until you are 70% full and chew your food well to allow your digestive juices to start breaking down your food.

Drink between meals and limit the amount of fluid you drink with food.

Chinese medicine divides foods into five flavors, each of which is associated with a different organ in the body.

BITTER

(heart and small intestine)

These cool the body and are used to stimulate the digestion, cool fevers, and clear bowel problems. They should only be used in small quantities.

Asparagus
Beer
Broccoli
Celery
Chicory
Coffee
Lettuce
Radish
Turnip
Watercress

SWEET
(stomach and spleen)

In moderation, sweet foods are a tonic, but a craving for them indicates a problem with the stomach or spleen.

Apple
Apricot
Barley
Beef
Carrot
Cheese
Chicken
Citrus fruit
Coffee
Mushroom
Milk
Oats

Peach
Peanuts
Pear
Plum
Pork
Potato
Raspberry
Rice
Spinach
Sugar
Tomato
Wine

PUNGENT

(lung and large intestine)

These disperse obstructions in the blood and enhance energy but should only be taken in small quantities.

Black pepper
Cayenne
Cabbage
Cherry
Chili
Garlic
Mint
Mustard
Nutmeg
Peppermint
Rosemary
Watercress

SALTY

(kidney and bladder)

These foods clear excess water
from the system, but should not
be taken to excess.

Barley
Crab
Duck
Ham
Lobster
Millet
Mussel
Oyster
Pork
Salt
Sardine
Seaweed

SOUR

(liver and gall bladder)

These foods are astringent and help prevent urinary incontinence, diarrhea, and excessive sweating.

Adzuki beans
Blackberry
Blackcurrant
Gooseberry
Grapefruit
Green leafy vegetables
Olive
Pomegranate
Sour plums
Tomato
Trout
Vinegar

Poor eating habits will affect our health physically, mentally, and spiritually. A good diet gives us a feeling of well-being and energy. We can now afford to eat foods every day that our ancestors were only able to have on festive occasions—but this does not mean that it is good and healthy to do so.

"Live neither in the entanglements of outer things, nor in the inner feeling of emptiness. Be serene in the oneness of things and such erroneous views will disappear by themselves."

Kanchi Sosan Hsin Hsin Ming